frozen earth

haiku by

Anne Elise Burgevin

frozen earth

ISBN 978-1-947271-16-6

Red Moon Press
PO Box 2461
Winchester VA
22604-1661 USA
www.redmoonpress.com

Cover photograph by Gerald Lang and
Jennifer Anne Tucker
American Chestnut Foundation's
Restoration project. Image of Tyler seeds.

first printing

Dedicated to my parents

Jules and Patti Burgevin

for nurturing my love
of writing and nature.

One winter's day an explosion rocked my neighborhood. I frantically searched for an explanation. War . . . earthquake. Then I saw a plume of smoke and knew someone's house was on fire. As a volunteer fireman's daughter, I ran to the scene only to discover my neighbor's house engulfed in flames. He was standing outside and was safe. Fire trucks arrived and the firemen and women quickly got to work. With nothing to do but watch, I soon realized they were spraying almost as much water on the adjacent houses as they were on the fire. I thought to myself how fortunate that the day is windless . . .

frozen earth still air
the fire doesn't jump houses

earth

nightfall
an orchid's
soft landing

another chance
to know the ordinary
winter meadow

at the picnic
my baby's bare tummy
the main attraction

lost in the apple blossoms song sparrow

low clusters
of black raspberries
her hidden talent

to soothe
the winter blues
tulips

shallow eddies
we came of age
on this river

paring down
her to-do list
autumn crickets

a small green apple
in the damp grass
you are leaving again

mint
patches
of
blue
feelings

plum season
all of a sudden
shorter mornings

buckwheat flowers
her fertile days
feel numbered

winter apples
she thinks
he's a keeper

clover
lover
over

blue petals her tell-all eyes

milkweed
the soft underside
of an afternoon

fallen fruit
his stump speech
on the sidewalk

March mud
our slippery race
relations

cultivated
wild rice
her smile

weeding
an excuse
to smell the flowers

apple blossoms
the ballerina
holds her pose

sprays of forsythia
at the backdoor
a lone traveler

knowing it will be
his last spring
wisteria tendrils

on occasion
grocery store flowers . . .
early spring

weeding
what my hands
know by heart

toad lilies
when all is said
and done

air

an orchid blossom drops his voice softens

solstice dawn
she gives the curtains
another tug

a mockingbird
falls silent
New Years Day

feng shui
facing the bluebird house
toward sunrise

first birth
from the narrows
an oriole's song

hummingbird nest
I was once
so small

her last day
flutters of
mourning cloaks

first frost
I give everything
to the night sky

truststardust

last light —
Venus
our homeward star

tufted titmouse
keeps nominating
springtime

turning a deaf ear
to the autumn wind
pink dahlias

drowsy wasp
three generations
of dusty letters

snow, rain
mud, wind
stone Buddha

fledge
ledge
edge

an owl calls
another answers
her change of heart

white petals
my neighbor's litter
everywhere

black ice
crows overtake us
on the bend

bald eagle
now a few heartbeats
and fields away

morning light
enveloped by
a snow squall

ripe fruit
falling into
your lap

laughing gulls
my hair loosens
in the breeze

fox sparrow
seeing things
in the snow

blue sky in unexpected places memories of you

spring thaw
a kite string
of geese

leaves
shading leaves
shading me

at the tree line
the wind and I
change course

cooler air
where the road dips
a late day moon

lingering moonlight
the comfort
of early dawn

Acknowledgments

"frozen earth" *Modern Haiku* 42.2; "nightfall" *bottle rockets* 29; "another chance" *brass bell* February 2017; "at the picnic" *Frogpond* 33.3; "lost" *Modern Haiku* 45.3; "low clusters" *Frogpond* 35.3; "to soothe" *hedgerow* 109; "shallow eddies" *Frogpond* 36.2; "paring down" *Modern Haiku* 46.1; "a small green apple" *Frogpond* 33.1; "mint patches" *Frogpond* 39.1; "plum season" *brass bell* November 2015; "buckwheat flowers" *Frogpond* 35.3; "winter apples" HNA Anthology 2015; "clover" *Modern Haiku* 48.3; "blue petals" *Modern Haiku* 43.3; "milkweed" *hedgerow* Spring print issue 2017; "fallen fruit" *Lakeview International Journal of Literature and Arts* 2; "March mud" *Modern Haiku* 47.3; "cultivated" *Modern Haiku* 45.1; "weeding" *Modern Haiku* 40.2; "apple blossoms" *The Heron's Nest* XIV:3; "sprays of forsythia" United Nations International School Contest 2017 (English Teachers Category) HM; "knowing it will be" *Frogpond* 35.2; "on occasion" UNIS Contest 2015 HM; "weeding"

The Heron's Nest XIX:3; "toad lilies" *Frogpond* 37.2; "an orchid" *Modern Haiku* 42.3; "solstice dawn" *Modern Haiku* 45.2; "a mocking bird" *Modern Haiku* 44.3; "feng shui" UNIS Contest 2016 HM; "first birth" *Beechwood Review* 1; "hummingbird" *Beechwood Review* 1; "her last day" *Modern Haiku* 43.3; "first frost" *Frogpond* 36.2; "trustardust" *Lakeview International Journal of Literature and Arts* 2; "last light" *Modern Haiku* 48.2; "tufted titmouse" *Frogpond* 38.3; "turning" *Modern Haiku* 44.1; "drowsy" *The Heron's Nest* XIV:4; "snow, rain" *hedgerow* 109; "fledge" *Modern Haiku* 48.3; "an owl calls" *Modern Haiku* 41.2; "white petals" *Modern Haiku* 45.3; "black ice" UNIS Contest 2016 2nd place; "bald eagle" *Modern Haiku* 47.2; "morning light" UNIS Contest 2017 HM; "ripe fruit" *Modern Haiku* 47.1; "laughing gulls" *Frogpond* 38.2; "fox sparrow" Anita Sadler Weiss Memorial Award 2013 HM; "blue sky" *Modern Haiku* 46.1; "spring thaw" *Modern Haiku* 46.2; "leaves" *Modern Haiku* 46.3; "at the tree line" UNIS Contest 2017 1st place; "cooler air" *Modern Haiku*, 48.1, 2017; "lingering moonlight" *hedgerow* 122, 2017).

ANNE BURGEVIN is a teacher, poet, naturalist and environmentalist. Throughout her life she has fostered awareness and a sense of wonder in her children and students about the natural world. While growing up in the Finger Lakes of central New York and then raising her children in the Seven Mountains region of central Pennsylvania, she has come to know and love the northeastern deciduous forests, and the lakes and rivers that shape and define these regions. Her haiku are an expression of her passion and concern for every living being, for whom she has deep regard, including weeds. Standing near a clump of seven foot Joe-pye weed in her yard one summer's day, Anne's neighbor told her, "Your yard looks wild and untended," which Anne took as a compliment. Wild and untended are key words in Anne's world.